A Step-by-Step
Guide and Showcase

First published in the United States of America by Quarry
Books, an imprint of
Rockport Publishers, Inc.
33 Commercial Street
Gloucester, Massachusetts 01930-5089
Telephone: (978) 282-9590
Fax: (978) 283-2742

Distributed to the book trade and art trade in the United
States by
North Light Books, an imprint of
F & W Publications
1507 Dana Avenue
Cincinnati, Ohio 45207
Telephone: (800) 289-0963

Other distribution by
Rockport Publishers, Inc.
Gloucester, Massachusetts 01930-5089

ISBN 1-56496-315-2

10 9 8 7 6 5 4 3 2

Design: Jennifer Ray
Production: Beth Santos

Front cover photos: *Melon Pitcher* by Steven Hill,
photo by Al Surratt.

Back cover photos: (top left) Photo by Joseph Molinaro;
(top right) *Copper Green Carved Vase* by Jim Connell,
photo by Paula Smith; (bottom right) *Raised Square Platter*
by Suze Lindsay, photo by Tom Mills.

Front flap photo: *Oval Footed Platter with Lateral Leaves*
by Linda Arbuckle. Photo by Linda Arbuckle.

This page: *Donut Bottle* by Michael Simon, photo by
Walker Montgomery.

See page 140 for complete list of interior photo credits.

Printed in China

Acknowledgments

First and foremost, I would like to thank the
artists included in this book. They were all
exceptionally patient and helpful. In addition,
many thanks to Joseph Molinaro, who
provided me with the information and photos
for the section on the potters of Jatun Molino.

Thanks also to the artists who sent images of
their fine work for the galleries. There was
simply not enough room to include all the work
I had to choose from, and many examples of
quality work had to be passed up.

Writing this, my first book, has been an
incredible learning experience, and I thank the
people at Rockport Publishers, especially
Shawna Mullen and Martha Wetherill, who
graciously led me through the entire process.

Last, I would like to thank two of my teachers:
Pat Everitt, who taught me about writing; and
Chris Staley, who taught me so much about
pots. I am their perpetual student.

Contents

Tall Persian Jar with Fish Decoration

by **MICHAEL SIMON**

Stoneware, salt-fired
15" x 9" (38 cm x 23 cm)

Preface

Language is an ever-changing tool. Even when we try to be precise and respectful, there is a danger that we may miscommunicate simply because of the fluid nature of language.

I know a young potter who gets irate when the terms *chalice* and *goblet* are used interchangeably or differently from the way she uses them. I attribute this, for the most part, to her age and inexperience. Most veteran potters know that many hours that would be better spent working in the studio can easily be wasted in debates over semantics. For this reason, many have grown weary of the "art versus craft" debate. I certainly include myself in that group. I have my own definitions of *art*, *craft*, *pottery*, and *ceramics*.

I seldom find cause to defend or explain my personal vocabulary. But as author of this book, perhaps an explanation of what was considered for inclusion under the title *Creative Pottery* is appropriate. For the purposes of this book, I have chosen to include two distinct types of work in clay. The first is work that is functional—intended to be used. This is work that extends a tradition stretching back to the earliest stages of human civilization. The other type of "pottery" is work that celebrates that tradition—without becoming a part of it. These are pots about pots. They may have all the right parts in all the right places. They might have a volume, a lid, a handle, and a spout. The difference lies in the intent of the work.

Introduction

If you hand a child a lump of clay, chances are you won't have to tell him or her what to do with it. Pinching, poking, rolling, and squishing, the child will almost certainly make something out of the clay—and something else and something else again—until the clay dries out or an adult intervenes.

Clay is the most fascinating and seductive material on earth. Wet and cool, soft and plastic; more tempting than a Siren; clay just begs to be shaped. Of course, as adults with the need to be productive, potters hone their skills through years of work in an effort to create objects of use and beauty.

As seductive and sensuous as clay can be, it is equally mysterious and complex. How many lifetimes would it take to unveil all its secrets? It is impossible to say. Perhaps because of this, it is a long-standing tradition of the craft that potters share information and help each other along. Generally speaking, potters are teachers—by nature, if not by profession. Painters give lectures. Potters give workshops. A potter who will not share information is often not trusted. Through this book, nine potters will have the opportunity to be your teachers, sharing the tools, materials, and techniques that have worked well for them.

I remember telling a musician friend of mine that the thing I really enjoyed about pottery was that it could last for thousands and thousands of years—or it could shatter in an instant. He replied, "So it's strong, yet fragile—like people." Somehow, the analogy that he seized on in a moment had escaped me for years. And that connection between pottery and people is at the heart of what potters do and why.

I have many, many pots in my home, which I use daily. None of them is my own, and this does not strike me as odd. To use a handmade pot is to participate in a dialogue with the maker. Using my own pots would be like talking to myself. But when I use a pot made by another person, I feel a connection to him or her, whether through simple admiration of skills or through fond memories of a moment shared. One would only have to open my kitchen cupboard to discover what I value, and which potters I admire and respect. By opening this book, you have opened that cupboard.

FORMING

Nesting Batter Bowls

by CHRIS STALEY

Wheel-thrown, soda-fired porcelain
8" x 16" (20 cm x 41 cm)

FORMING

The potter's goal is not unlike the architect's—the aesthetic containment of space. And the means to that end are infinitely variable.

Many clay workers choose the potter's wheel. It is a quick way of stretching clay up into space and then shaping it into a pleasing form. The wheel offers the opportunity to reveal the silky, sensual nature of clay, as Chris Staley's porcelain cups illustrate. But "throwing" requires years of practice to gain competency; decades to really master.

Other potters choose to "hand-build," without use of the potter's wheel. Pinching, coiling, working with slabs, as well as carving clay, are ancient approaches to the material and predate the potter's wheel. Yet contemporary potters, such as Lana Wilson, still evoke new visions and forms using these ancient methods. Wilson's slab-built teapots are both whimsical and dignified, and they celebrate the tactile qualities of clay.

Clay may also be formed by using molds. Called "slip-casting," this approach is best suited to the creation of a large number of identical forms and is often used in manufacturing. Slip-casting can provide consistent, repeatable forms, but it amplifies the need for an infusion of personality or "spirit" in order to make the work appear truly creative.

Becoming fluent in all these methods of forming with clay frees the potter to make real and solid any vision of form. For example, Michael Simon first raises a form on the potter's wheel, but then he applies many methods of the hand-builder to achieve his signature style.

Wheels, molds, slabs, coils—they are all simply the tools potters use for forming and transforming base clay into beautiful and, perhaps, useful objects.

Ceremonial Teapot

by LANA WILSON

White stoneware
9" high x 17" long x 4" wide
(23 cm x 43 cm x 10 cm)

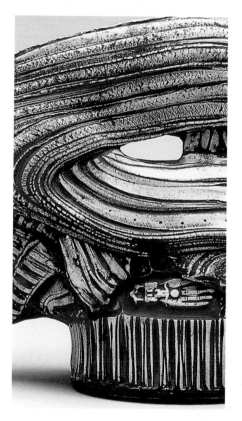

Donut Bottle

by MICHAEL SIMON

Wheel-thrown, stoneware, salt-fired
8" (22.3 cm) high

Teapots

by FRANK FABENS

Slip cast
7" high x 5" wide x 3" deep (18 cm x 13 cm x 8 cm)

"My desire to expand my repertoire of lidded forms led me to this squared, roofed jar. Over the years it has evolved, but continues to intrigue me."

—Michael Simon

MAKING A SQUARE COVERED JAR

Many years ago, when Brancusi declined to remain and work in Rodin's studio, he explained his decision by saying, "Nothing can grow in the shade of a mighty oak." Many contemporary potters in Europe and the United States have struggled to find their beam of light in the mighty shadow of Bernard Leach, especially if they were trained in his tradition.

Michael Simon started his pottery career at the University of Minnesota, learning his craft from Warren MacKenzie, Leach's first American apprentice. Influenced by the Leach tradition through his teacher, Simon has long strived to make modest, useful pots that are also inexpensive. His unique style appears to be both simple and direct, as well as sophisticated and elegant. Forms often begin on the wheel and are then altered into squares, triangles, and rectangles. Today, many years after leaving Minnesota and moving to the Athens, Georgia, area, Simon's pots still reflect the dignity and simplicity that Leach exalted. They also show a variety of other influences, including ancient Persian ceramics.

SHAPING UP:
Squaring the Circle

One of Simon's most intriguing forms is the thrown, squared, and lidded Persian Jar. Like all of his work, the form begins on the wheel. Simon prefers using a Leach treadle wheel, in part because of its uneven rotation, which produces a slightly imperfect form. After the base of the jar—a simple, flat-bottomed cylinder—is thrown, the diameter of the opening is measured for a lid. Corners are made on the cylinder by pushing out from within with one finger so that the walls are gradually stretched to form a rectangular shape. The base will be paddled at various stages of dryness until the edges are crisp and sharp.

Tools

• large, flat wooden paddles

• long, thin-bladed steel knife

• calipers

• trimming tools

• fettling knife

A simple cylinder is thrown with a flat bottom and vertical walls. Simon measures the inside diameter of the opening with a pair of calipers. He will use this measurement later to determine the diameter of the inside edges, or flange, of the lid.

The calipers are set aside, and he determines the placement of four corners on the form. These corners are started by running a finger up the interior wall, pushing outward slightly to stretch and thin the wall.

Simon throws a lid with a very thick edge. A short flange, which will hold the lid in place, is pulled up and, using the caliper measurement taken earlier, matched in diameter to that of the base opening. The corners of the flange are created the same way they were on the base, using a finger to push out the wall at the proper place. Simon "eyeballs" the placement of the corners by looking at the nearby base.

When the pot dries to a "soft," leather-hard stage, Simon paddles it to flatten the planes of the form and to sharpen and define the corners. The top edge of the base is paddled first.

The base is flipped over so that the entire wall can be paddled flat. Note that this flattening of the walls causes the floor to compress and buckle. By tapping in the floor of the jar slightly early in the paddling process, Simon directs this buckling inward.

Next, the lid of the jar is trimmed while the lid is not quite leather hard, because after it is trimmed, he continues to manipulate it to define the corners of the flange. Simon leaves a slight peak in the center but maintains most of the thickness of the edge.

⊚ Holding the lid against his body, Simon compresses the sides of the lid in order to square the flange. He repeats this process for all four corners.

⊚ The round, thick lid with the squared flange is fitted onto the base of the jar and adjusted to fit.

⊚ Simon approaches the pot from above and marks where the corners should be. With one long, confident movement, he cuts the edge of the lid from above, following the contour of the rectangular jar below. The entire pot is turned as each successive side of the lid is cut. Much of the weight of the lid is shed as Simon finishes the process of squaring the lid.

Cut edges are softened slightly with a wet finger or sponge. The lid is then paddled to create four planes, implying a kind of "roof" for the jar.

Finally, the pot is elevated with four added feet. With the lid removed, the base is flipped over and the bottom of the jar is scored at the corners. Simon cuts a thick coil of clay into four "slugs" about 1" (3 cm) long and adds them to the corners.

When the added feet are leather hard, the pot is turned upright. The feet are then cut with a long, thin knife on the outside planes to conform with the overall feeling of the pot. To make an even cut, Simon trims the two feet on each side of the jar at once, with one stroke of the knife.

Cutting the added feet continues around the pot, giving each foot a sharp corner. The finished Persian Jar is decorated with slips and salt-fired at stoneware temperatures.

Notes from the Studio

To make lidded square pots, keep in mind the following tips.

> Simon admits that it took him a long time to realize that the trick to making lids fit on square forms was a relatively simple matter. When the jar and the lid are still round on the wheel, measurements are taken with calipers. When the two pieces are later squared, they should still fit. In the end, it is a matter of trusting measurements and knowing that the process works.

> By stretching the wall at the corners of the base of the pot, you not only determine where the corners will be, but you also make it easier to manipulate the form later in the process.

> Squaring the circular lid in Simon's Persian Jar takes a sharp knife, a steady hand, and a good amount of nerve. The clay should not be hacked at or whittled away. One long, confident cut is best.

"I often use the symbol of the hand in my work.

In some cultures, the hand means friendship,

and in others, it signifies protection. To me, it is

a symbol of the joy of working with one's hands."

—Lana Wilson

MAKING A SLAB TEAPOT

California artist Lana Wilson creates slab vessels, rich in texture and gesture, using a number of handmade stamps, as well as a variety of other tools, to enrich the surface of her pots. With an endless assortment of surface textures to choose from, Wilson has chosen to focus on the symbols of past and present cultures and subcultures to add meaning to her work.

The symbolic graffiti left by hobos during the Depression of the 1930s are just such symbols.
Hobos around the world would leave symbolic graffiti as messages for other hobos. "Don't give
up," or "Food and money given here," were some of the messages represented by simple,
geometric marks and understood by members of a vast subculture. Those symbols, as well as
others from many other cultures, intrigue Wilson, who incorporates them into her hand-built
pottery forms. Her intent is to demonstrate the importance of ritual and symbols in our lives.

CREATING DECORATIVE SLABS

Impressing Textures and Raising Designs

Lana Wilson makes her own stamps by carving on leather-hard clay, by pressing small objects into soft clay, and by combining these techniques. Stamps can be made out of any clay and bisque-fired to make them durable and porous. Jewelry, kitchen utensils, and shop tools can be used to make great stamps. The image you carve or press into the stamp will create a mirror image when it is used, so reverse letters, numbers, and some symbols.

To make a slab with a raised design, Wilson uses a method she calls "dropping." Sketch out a design on a piece of paper larger than the slab of clay. Place thin coils and small balls of clay on the paper in the sketched pattern. Lay a thin, soft slab of clay over it. Pick up the piece of paper carefully and drop it several times on a clean, flat surface. The slab "hugs" the clay design underneath. The bits of clay can stay imbedded in the clay or be removed.

Tools

- variety of rolling pins (one smooth; others textured)

- pony roller (a small, double-ended rolling tool)

- bisque-fired clay stamps

- fettling knife (or craft knife)

- hibachi sticks

- paper clay and magic water (see Recipes for Slips)

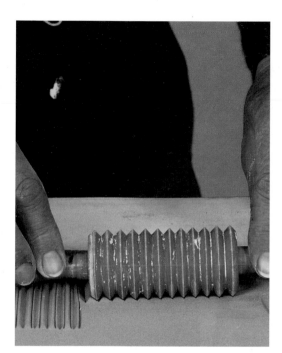

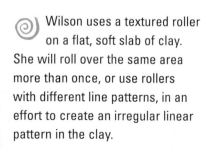 Wilson uses a textured roller on a flat, soft slab of clay. She will roll over the same area more than once, or use rollers with different line patterns, in an effort to create an irregular linear pattern in the clay.

Next Wilson uses a variety of bisqued clay stamps, which she made, to imprint the same clay slab. Some of the stamps represent symbols of the hobo subculture; some, other cultures. She also uses several stamps of hands, a symbol that has many meanings.

When the rectangular slab of clay is textured to her liking, Wilson joins two edges together to create a cylinder. The seam is rolled flat from within using a section of broom handle. The slab cylinder is then stood up on end and made into an oval. The bottom edge of the cylinder is scored and a slab bottom is added. Wilson uses paper clay or magic water whenever she joins pieces.

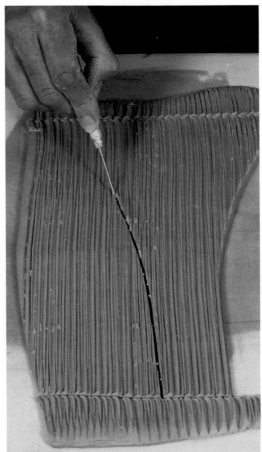

Wilson joins the two long sides of the spout, using a hibachi stick inside for support. The pony roller is used to secure the joint. No scoring is needed because the clay is still very soft. Wilson sometimes uses a blow dryer to stiffen the spout before attaching it to the body of the pot.

After the bottom slab has been attached, beveled, and smoothed with a small roller, Wilson sets the cylinder upright on a piece of paper to keep it from sticking to the table on which she is working. She then gently, but firmly, pinches together the top of the cylinder, making sure that the pot retains a soft, convex shape.

Creating and adding a spout to the form is the next step. Wilson textures a slab of soft clay, just as she did to create the body of the vessel. From this slab, she cuts a long, triangular shape with sides curving inward. The curved edges are beveled with the pony roller so that when they are joined, no ridge will form.

After deciding the proper placement of the spout and scoring both pot and spout, the two pieces are joined using paper-clay slip. Wilson sometimes leaves the hibachi stick in the spout for added support. She "skewers" the pot with the stick, which she removes when the spout is leather hard.

For the teapot handle, a slab of very soft clay is rolled out and textured. Wilson then cuts a long, triangular shape similar to the slab for the spout, but with straight sides. She gently turns the slab over so that the texture is on the outside and then folds its long edges in toward the center. What is created is akin to a flattened ice cream cone.

The small end of the flattened cone is then looped over and attached to the wide end to create a basic handle loop.

◎ The loop for the handle is flattened and made larger by being thrown onto a flat surface. Wilson at first throws the slab straight down. This first throw firms and thickens the clay and allows her to retain the hole at the center of the loop.

◎ A series of diagonal "slaps" of the clay on the table stretch and spread the slab. Wilson must often stretch several slabs in this manner to get two that work well together to form a single handle. She "performs a little plastic surgery" to fit the slabs together and then scores and attaches them to the sides of the teapot, using paper clay as a binding slip (see Notes from the Studio on the next page).

◎ The lid for the teapot is made the same way the handle was made, but with slightly larger slabs. Wilson prefers the lid to extend across the entire top of the form, connecting spout and handle.

The finished (unfired) ceremonial teapot. After bisquing, Wilson brushes on glaze and fires to cone 6. When the teapot is cool, she brushes on a contrasting glaze, wiping it off the raised texture so that it stays only in the recesses. The pot is then refired to cone 06.

Notes from the Studio

Wilson uses these recipes to join edges, attach pieces to the slab, and for mending.

> Wilson makes "paper clay" to mend cracks and holes in green or bisqued ware, as well as for a binder when attaching pieces together. The advantage of paper clay is that it can be used even as the pot dries. To make it, simply measure by volume one part paper lint (or toilet paper) and three parts dry clay. Mix with plenty of water, using a hand mixer. After it is blended, pour off the excess water and store in an airtight container.

> To glue together separate pieces, Wilson uses a bonding recipe that she calls "magic water." Add 3 tablespoons liquid sodium silicate and 1.5 teaspoons soda ash to one gallon of water and mix well. Liquid sodium silicate is also called "egg keep" and can be found at some drugstores. Ceramic suppliers also carry liquid sodium silicate.

"For me, the essence of making pots is about being human. It's about strength and fragility. It's about the intimate moment when the hand touches the handle of a cup. It's about making what is not there compelling."

—Chris Staley

MAKING CUPS

Chris Staley has attained fame in the ceramics world by making large, faceted vases and bowls. Ignoring the delicate implications of porcelain, he handles the material aggressively, working large and thick; tearing and cutting the pure white clay and then salt-firing it with luscious glazes. Not long ago, though, Staley was drawn to making smaller, more utilitarian objects. Cups, batter bowls, dinner plates, and covered jars intrigued him not only with their aesthetic challenges but also with their sociological and philosophical statements. "In our technologically oriented and cost-effective world, handmade pottery isn't necessary," Staley explains. "Yet, something compels me to continue on in this ancient tradition."

"The oldest cup was someone's hands held together to bring water to his lips," begins an essay Chris Staley wrote not long ago, "How a Handmade Cup Can Save the World." In the essay, Staley muses over the relevance of making cups and other useful vessels in our modern, technological society. An intelligent, thoughtful, and sensitive man, he struggles to bring meaning and purpose to everything he does—and to every pot he makes. Sometimes fluid, sometimes formal, Staley's cups can vary greatly in feeling. All, though, reflect his touch—his unique way of handling the material.

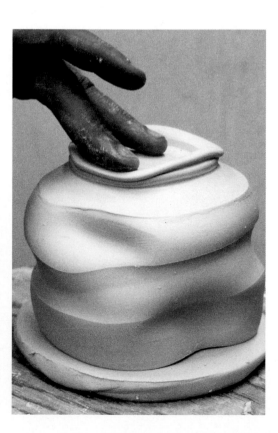

SETTING UP:
Preparing Porcelain

Most potters choose to work with porcelain because of its pure color and translucent quality. Porcelain, when fired to appropriately high temperatures, "rings" if tapped, and if it is thin enough, light can pass through the wall of a porcelain pot. Staley not only celebrates these qualities of porcelain but also is intrigued by its strength and strata, sometimes twisting and tearing the clay to reveal both its grace and structure.

Because it is the most pure and therefore the least plastic of clay bodies, porcelain can be very difficult to control and manipulate on the wheel. One way to add plasticity to porcelain is to let it "age" for as long as possible between the time it is mixed wet and the time it is thrown. This allows the water in the porcelain to surround each clay particle and may also promote the growth of bacteria, both of which add to its plasticity.

Tools

- variety of small flexible metal ribs

- trimming tools

- cut-off wire

- wooden modeling tool

- chamois

- signature stamp

Staley uses a flexible metal rib to smooth and shape the clay while throwing. He prefers these tools because he can bend and flex them to achieve the exact curve he wants the cup to take. He can choose from an assortment of flexible ribs of various sizes and shapes.

Staley starts to square the cups immediately after he throws them, by drawing a finger up the interior wall, pushing out as he goes.

After the cups have been squared and allowed to dry just a little, Staley uses a variety of ribs and other tools to make impressions in the walls of each cup. The clay is soft enough at this point to bend and give under slight pressure, but not so wet that it is sticky. Staley must support the wall from within during this altering process.

After the clay has dried to leather hard and a foot has been trimmed, Staley emphasizes the corners by adding a small coil of clay to the exterior wall, blending it in by hand. He then refines this augmented corner by scraping and smoothing the edge with the flexible metal ribs. By approaching the problem in this way, Staley is able to maintain a "soft" corner inside the cup while creating a sharp edge on the exterior.

 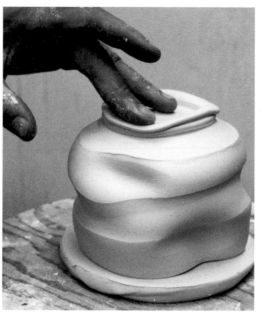

When making softer, more fluid cups, Staley begins by throwing a basic cup shape, thinning the walls, and creating the volume. As a final step of the throwing process, Staley twists and alters the form by using the metal ribs on the outside wall and a supporting hand on the inside. His goal is to create torque in the form and fluid lines in the "skin" of the cup, without losing the structural integrity of the form.

Cups with uneven lips are trimmed on a thick pad of soft clay. Staley likes to trim cups while they are still a little wet. After the excess clay has been removed, he can manipulate the foot, softening and altering it to relate to the rest of the cup.

When pulling a handle for cups, Staley considers how the width of the handle relates to the space between the knuckles of the fingers. Will it be a comfortable fit for the user?

A cup is dipped in a bucket of porcelain slip. This slip coating gives a final soft, clean skin to the unfired cup.

Notes from the Studio

To help you with your own soft, manipulated, and smooth-surfaced cups, follow Chris Staley's advice.

> Altering a thrown form usually creates an uneven lip, which can make trimming a foot tricky business. To solve the problem of trimming a pot with an uneven lip, Staley uses a thick pad of the same clay as a base to trim on. The cup is turned upside-down and its lip is gently eased into the thick, soft pad until the bottom is level.

> To make a deflocculated porcelain slip that gives a thick, workable skin to a leather-hard pot, Staley starts with the same porcelain body he uses for throwing. He fills a five-gallon bucket about halfway with small chunks of dried clay, adds enough water to cover, and lets it soak overnight. Excess water is poured off and the clay is mixed using a power drill with a mixing attachment. When the mixture is smooth, Staley adds one to two tablespoons of sodium silicate to one cup of warm water, which he blends into the slip using the power mixer. Staley lays this "thixatropic" slip onto the pot by hand and smoothes it with a flexible metal rib.

> When using any deflocculated clay slip, it is very important to ensure that it does not get mixed back into the throwing clay reclaim. Once deflocculated, its properties will interfere with the clay's workability on the wheel.

GALLERY OF FORMS

> *Ritual Teapot*

by LANA WILSON

Hand-built with soft slabs, white stoneware fired in electric kiln
9" (23 cm) high

v *Altar Teapot*

by LANA WILSON

Hand-built with soft slabs, white stoneware fired in electric kiln
7" (18 cm) high

> *Donut Bottle*

by MICHAEL SIMON

Wheel-thrown, stoneware, salt-fired
8" (22.3 cm) high

^ *Teapots*

by NICK JOERLING

Wheel-thrown and altered, stoneware
3" wide x 11.5" high x 7" long (29 cm x 8 cm x 18 cm)

^ *Two Cups*

by MICHAEL SIMON

Wheel-thrown, stoneware, salt-fired
4" (21.8 cm) high

> *Cream & Sugar & Tray*

by NICK JOERLING

Thrown and altered, stoneware tray
6" wide x 2" high x 11" long (5 cm x 15 cm x 28 cm)

> *Black Clay Covered Jar*

by CHRIS STALEY

Wheel-thrown and altered, black stoneware
20" (51 cm) high

^ *Nesting Batter Bowls*

by CHRIS STALEY

Wheel-thrown, soda-fired porcelain
8" x 16" (20 cm x 41 cm)

> *Tall B Vase*

by FRANK FABENS

Slip cast
13" (33 cm) high

> *Teapot*

by FRANK FABENS

Slip cast
7" high x 5" wide x 3" deep (18 cm x 13 cm x 8 cm)

^ *Vase Form with Rope Lip and Foot*

by SALLY PORTER

Earthenware with vitreous engobes, clay-coated
fiber mesh
11.5" (29 cm) high

< *Oval Vase Form*

by SALLY PORTER

Earthenware with vitreous engobes, clay-coated
fiber mesh
11" high x 14" long (28 cm x 36 cm)

> *Ritual Teapot*

by LANA WILSON

White stoneware
8" high x 15" long x 4" wide (20 cm x 38 cm x 10 cm)

^ *Tree Trunk Teapot*

by AH-LEON

Hand-built, stoneware
16.5" high x 12.5" long (42 cm x 32 cm)

> *Ceremonial Bowl*

by LANA WILSON

White stoneware
7" high x 5" diameter (18 cm x 13 cm)

^ *Ceremonial Teapot*

by LANA WILSON

White stoneware
9" high x 17" long x 4" wide (23 cm x 43 cm x 10 cm)

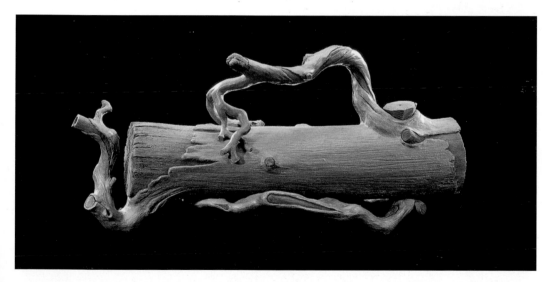

^ *Tree Trunk Teapot*

by AH-LEON

Hand-built, stoneware
11.5" high x 24.8" long (29 cm x 63 cm)

> *Wood Block Teapot*

by AH-LEON

Hand-built, stoneware
17.5" high x 20" long (44 cm x 51 cm)

< Pitcher with Pulled Lip

by MICHAEL SIMON

Stoneware, salt-fired
10" x 6" (25 cm x 15 cm)

> Tall Persian Jar with Fish Decoration

by MICHAEL SIMON

Stoneware, salt-fired
15" x 9" (38 cm x 23 cm)

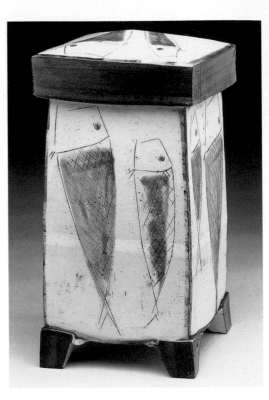

> Four Cups

by CHRIS STALEY

Soda-fired, stoneware
3" (8 cm) high

< *Square Covered Jar*

by CHR1S STALEY

Soda-fired, stoneware
6" x 10" (15 cm x 25 cm)

< *Four Cups*

by CHR1S STALEY

Soda-fired, stoneware
3" (8 cm) high

Platter

by STEVEN HILL

Single-fired, stoneware
21" diameter (53 cm)

SURFACE

Mies van der Rohe once said,"God is in the details." What he failed to mention was that the Devil was there, too. Decorating pottery can be a difficult balancing act. The strongest surface decoration might rescue a weak form. But poor surface decoration can easily kill a strong form. A potter deals with the same visual considerations as any painter. Line, color, texture, and proportion are obvious concerns in making beautiful ware. But the potter has the added challenge of harmonizing the surface elements with the three-dimensional form on which they are presented. Because of this, it is somewhat misleading to deal with the surface as an entirely separate element. More often than not, a pot's surface is anticipated at the forming stage, and altered by the firing process.

Like every other part of the ceramic process, there is a lifetime of lessons to be learned and secrets to be revealed when it comes to dealing with the surface of a pot. Some potters take the "high-tech" road; some take the "low-tech" road. The science of glaze chemistry and calculation can be the delight or the frustration of the potter. And, oh, the dangers involved in picking up a brush!

If we focus on surface decoration as a distinct element, we find four basic categories of decoration: geometric, symbolic, structural, and natural (or from nature.) And each type of decoration has its own history, significance, tools, and techniques.

Although every potter must, at some point, deal with surface as an issue, the artists showcased in this section are recognized for their unique approaches and for consistently producing quality work that celebrates the surface.

Biscuit Jar with Lateral Leaves

by LINDA ARBUCKLE

Majolica
on terra-cotta
8.5" x 13" (22 cm x 33 cm)

Cypress Ewer

by STEVEN HILL

Single-fired stoneware;
Wheel-thrown and altered
17" x 11" (43 cm x 28 cm)

Teapot

by PETER PINNELL

Low-fired, with terra sigillata
and patina surface
4" x 6" x 5" (10 cm x 15 cm x 13 cm)

"It is important to begin at the point when the pot is being formed on the wheel in order to really understand my approach to the surface."

—Steven Hill

RAW GLAZING

Steven Hill has long been respected for the richness he achieves on the surfaces of his works. His pots are beautiful in photographs, and even more stunning in person. Using a varied palette of colors, playing matte surfaces against transparent, and building up thin layers of glazes on the form, Hill creates surfaces tht display startling depth. The viewer may ponder what is under the surface, on the surface, and reflecting off the surface.

Hill is one of the rare potters who apply glaze to the interior and exterior of works when they are completely dry and still "green," or unfired. This technique is called "raw glazing." He then fires the raw, glazed ware in a standard gas reduction kiln to cone 10–11, forgoing the bisquing stage altogether.

The economics of time and money play a role in his choice of single firing. And for potters working with "atmospheric" kilns—soda, salt, or anagama and noborigama—in which little or no glaze is applied to the pot before firing, allowing the atmosphere inside the kiln to work its magic, the only real advantage of bisque firing may be the ease of transporting the ware to the kiln. But for most potters, the dangers of foregoing a bisque firing far outweigh any advantages. Steven Hill has discovered how to sidestep the pitfalls.

The sense of a continuous flow of work is, for Hill, the greatest benefit of single firing. By eliminating the bisque firing, he does not have to reacquaint himself with the piece before dealing with the surface. Having achieved a certain sense of reliability with his glazing techniques, Hill can further integrate the form and the surface of his work.

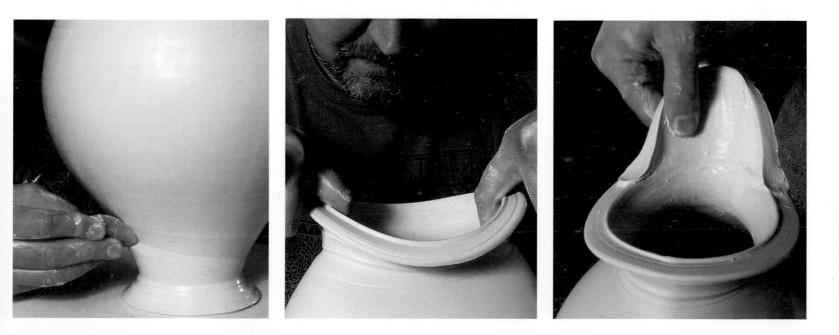

SETTING UP THE SURFACE—
Throwing a Melon Pitcher

When Steven Hill creates a melon pitcher, his primary concern is aesthetics. But he is also aware of the structural issues involved with single firing as he works on the wheel. Hill uses ribs to put a tight, smooth surface, or skin, on the form to emphasize the feeling of pressure from within. This tight skin also lessens the amount of water absorbed into the pot during glazing.

The potter is concerned with drawing the viewer's eye upward along the form and off the spout, like liquid. In forming the piece, Hill uses a wooden modeling tool to put a spiral in the neck, creating a sense of upward movement toward a spout that will be added later. Indentations are created by pressing into the wall with the edge of a wooden rib and dragging it down the form at angles to the foot. These indentations act as a corset, giving a feeling of voluptuousness and generosity to the pitcher.

Tools

- wooden modeling tool

- stainless steel scraper

- large syringe

- spray gun (for auto spray paint)

- small spray gun (for auto paint touch-ups)

- respirator

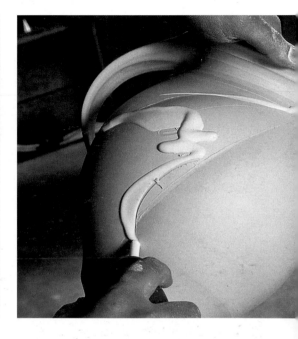

Shape strongly influences surface decoration, a fact Hill considers from the start. Using a stainless steel scraper, he creates a twisting line from the foot upward into the belly of the pitcher. Twisting at the bottom of the form is accentuated by pushing the wall of the pitcher out from inside on either side of the ribbed line.

A U-shaped spout and a handle are added when the lip is leatherhard. The spout is curved and refined so it will not only look elegant but pour well. A handle is pulled, attached, and refined. Notice the S-shaped curve that begins at the tip of the spout and continues across the rim and down the handle.

Lines of slip of varying thickness are trailed onto the leather-hard form with a syringe. Hill made some slight adjustments to a large, medical-supply syringe to make a comfortable slip-trailing tool. His goal is a finished line that is subtle rather than blatant, so he uses a very thick slip similar in color to the clay body. The pot is then allowed to dry thoroughly before being glazed.

When the pitcher is bone dry, glaze is poured into the interior. The pot is turned slowly and steadily (swishing the glaze a little to coat the entire inside wall), and the excess glaze is dumped out. The exterior of the pitcher will be sprayed with thin layers of glaze. Spraying the glaze significantly reduces the amount of water absorbed by the clay wall.

After the interior coating of glaze has dried, Hill (wearing a respirator for safety) applies the exterior base coat of glaze using a large automotive spray gun. To take pressure and strain off his elbow, Hill has rigged a counterweight for the large spray gun by using bungee cords anchored to the back wall of the spray booth.

After the sprayed base coat has dried, contrasting glazes are sprayed on certain areas to highlight the form and accentuate the visual movement of the pitcher. For this and subsequent steps, Hill uses a smaller spray gun designed for auto paint touchups. (This one is a DeVilbiss, model EGA.)

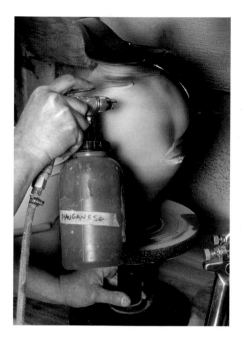

A final glaze of manganese saturate is applied to highlight the handle, spout, and lip, as well as selected other areas of the form. The finished work will be fired slowly in an oxidation atmosphere to bisque temperature, then heated to Cone 10–11 in a medium reduction atmosphere. At the end of the firing, Hill oxidizes the kiln for several minutes to "clean up" the atmosphere, which also brightens the colors of the glazes.

Notes from the Studio

For potters interested in single firing, Hill suggests you consider the following.

> First, the clay body needs a certain amount of dry strength to withstand the expansion and contraction caused when the glaze is applied.

> Also, *how* you throw is important. Compressing the walls and floor, avoiding thin spots in the wall, and throwing with little water will increase your chances for success when raw glazing.

> Finally, the ability of the glaze to shrink with the pot during the drying and firing is critical, so you must consider the amount of clay in your glazes.

"Majolica is a very honest, very unforgiving kind of pottery. If you didn't put it there before it goes into the kiln, it won't get any better in the firing. There are no gifts from the kiln gods."

—Linda Arbuckle

MAJOLICA DECORATION

Majolica is a traditional approach to pottery making in which earthenware is covered with a white, tin-opacified, viscous glaze and decorated by applying colorants on a raw glazed surface. The viscosity of the glaze restricts the flow as the glaze melts, giving a glossy surface that maintains the line quality of the surface decoration. The term *majolica* derives from the Spanish port of Majorca, from which the Italians imported the ware. When the French imported it from Faenza, they called the work "faience." Later, the Dutch perfected the techniques and called their work "Delftware," for the city that specialized in its creation.

Linda Arbuckle is a master of harmony in this difficult art. The majolica she creates is at once traditional and contemporary. Revealing a love for plant life that one expects from a former biology major, her pots are decorative and have a broad appeal. Yet they are complex in their marriage of form and surface. "Miss Linda" has worked with majolica surfaces for more than a quarter century. Recognized as a leading authority on the history, chemistry, and aesthetics of this centuries-old tin-glazed surface, Arbuckle has taught at Louisiana State University and the University of Florida.

SETTING UP:
Getting the Glaze Right

Majolica is very unforgiving, so it is important to take care at every step of the process. To get a good start, Arbuckle dampens the bisqued pot before dipping it into the white base glaze. This ensures that the glaze coating will not be too thick, which could lead to pinholing in the finished surface. Any lumps or drips on the glazed pot can be sanded off with fine sandpaper, or simply rubbed with a finger.

If the glaze wants to settle quickly in the bucket, Epsom salts can be added to keep the materials in suspension. Add one-half to three tablespoons of Epsom salts, mixed in hot water, per five gallons of glaze.

Tools

• assortment of fine and flat brushes

• banding wheel

• wax resist (colorless)

• black and colored overglaze stains

• sponge

• plastic palette, with wells for color mixing

After dipping the bowl into a white base glaze and allowing it to dry, Arbuckle lightly sands the surface of the bowl with fine sandpaper to remove drips and other imperfections. Doing this will provide an even finish on the fired work, as well as make decorating easier.

Once sanded, a soft, wide brush is used to remove any loose, powdered glaze from the surface of the bowl.

Majolica decoration requires that you start from the foreground and work back into the background. (Flowers, leaves, and background color will be applied in that order.) Arbuckle often "loads" the brush with two or more colors at once in an effort to achieve a softly blended and fluid stroke. Here, the petals surrounding the center of the flower are painted on.

 Once the base color of the flower has dried, Arbuckle applies black-line work to define the shapes and add contrast to the design.

 Layers of colors are added to build up a richness of surface. Here, red strokes are added to the yellow-orange petals of the flower.

 More black-line details may be added after each layer of color has dried.

Wax resist is carefully brushed on over the floral motif and allowed to dry. This is an important step in the progression of layers of the surface image. By protecting the image of the flower with a wax coating, Arbuckle is able to paint the next layer back without worrying about affecting the work she has already done.

The leaves behind the flower are added. Arbuckle again loads the brush with different colors of overglaze before laying in the leaf in a few strokes. The wax resist on the flower is clear, giving her an unobstructed view of her previous design.

The overglaze from the last stroke "beads" on the wax resist and must be carefully removed by dabbing with a small sponge.

  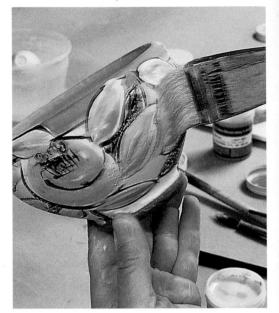

After each successive layer of color is brushed on, Arbuckle adds black lines for contrast and detail. A coat of wax resist follows the black lines at each step in the development of the design to protect the work that is already done.

With the entire flower motif protected by wax resist, background colors can be added. A blue band of color is added to the top and outlined in black when it dries. Arbuckle uses a banding wheel to apply a thin, straight black line. This blue band and outline will also be painted with wax resist after they dry.

Finally, a pink background for the middle section is brushed on, using a wider, flat brush.

Notes from the Studio

Arbuckle has developed these methods to enrich the majolica surface and to solve technical problems.

> Arbuckle often loads her brush, putting on more than one color before using it. Dip the brush in the predominant color first, then carefully dab other colors on it. Using more than one color on the brush at once can make a richer, more interesting brushstroke.

> White dotting on the colored areas is a common problem and may be caused by gases escaping from the clay or glaze during firing. Arbuckle has found that a thinner base coat of glaze and a slower firing help to prevent this problem.

> If the wax resist used over a glazed area begins to peel up from its edges, it may be a sign that the glazed surface was not free of dust. To prevent this from happening again, brush the glazed surface with a soft, flat brush to remove loose glaze.

> Peeling could also be a sign that the wax resist is too thick. Thin it with water. You can often remedy the peeling by gently heating the wax resist with a hair dryer and pushing it back down onto the surface.

"1 strive to give a sense of precision to my work, but not of a cold, mechanical nature. 1 prefer a more casual, fluid precision that reminds the viewer that the object was made by hand."

—Peter Pinnell

DECORATING A TEAPOT

Peter Pinnell relishes that particular kind of beauty found in objects that have survived many years of usefulness, such as a handrail on a stair or an ornament on a statue. Whether it is made of wood or metal, glass or clay, it takes on a patina over several years—a depth of surface that adds character. If it has been constantly used, it may be polished smooth by the touch of many hands.

Pinnell strives to recreate this polish and patina in his own work. "The surfaces I employ are intended to evoke this feeling: the sense that this is in some way a special object," he says. "The ornament acts as a focal point and is intended to entice the viewer to give my work closer scrutiny." The small scale of Pinnell's teapots also serves to draw the viewer close to the work. Once there, the richness of the surface and the delicacy of the detailing are revealed.

A master of clay and glaze chemistry, Pinnell most recently has been working with raised, intricate slip decorations and terra sigillata finishes. Terra sigillata, a slip make from the finest particles of clay, produces a smooth, tight skin on the surface of the pot. From a distance, these teapots look like tarnished silver services, but closer inspection reveals precise clay objects made with loving attention to detail.

SETTING UP:
Making the Teapot

The teapot is made from slabs of clay that were pounded out using the large paddle. Templates are used to cut the walls and the spout of the teapot, which are assembled when leather-hard. The walls are scored and slipped, then paddled with the smaller paddle to make a secure joint. Once the teapot is assembled, its edges are sharpened using a "Sure-form" tool. Cut edges, on the other hand, are softened with a foam eye shadow applicator. Pinnell uses a large spatula to add texture, and a bamboo scraper to create the gallery or seat for the lid. Holes are cut in the teapot wall and the spout is added. Finally, a smaller hole, called a "steam hole," is cut into the lid to aid in a smooth pour.

Tools

• liquid food coloring

• detailing brush

• bulb syringe

• spattering tool (or old toothbrush)

• rubber brayer

• wide, soft brush (*hake* brush)

A grid is brushed onto the surface of the leather-hard pot using food coloring. This makes it easier to apply a pattern, especially on complex forms. The food coloring will burn off completely. (Ink sometimes contains metals that will remain after firing.) For more complex patterns, Pinnell sometimes uses one color to lay out the grid on the pot and another color to test portions of the pattern he will use.

Using a bulb syringe, Pinnell trails a repeating pattern of slip onto the pot. The trailing slip is made from the same clay used for the pot, except it is thinned down and run through a 50-mesh screen.

⊚ To achieve a fuzzy or corroded look to the surface, he spatters slip onto the pot using a spattering tool designed specifically for that purpose. An old toothbrush works just about as well.

⊚ The pattern and texture are then rolled or pressed down using a printmakers' rubber brayer. The rolling changes the shape of the trailed slip, exaggerates the thick-to-thin nature of the lines, and achieves the line quality of a three-dimensional brushstroke.

⊚ After the pot is dry, Pinnell then coats it with terra sigillata and polishes it with his fingertips. He uses a wide, soft hake brush to apply the terra sigillata, but it can also be applied by spraying, pouring, or dipping.

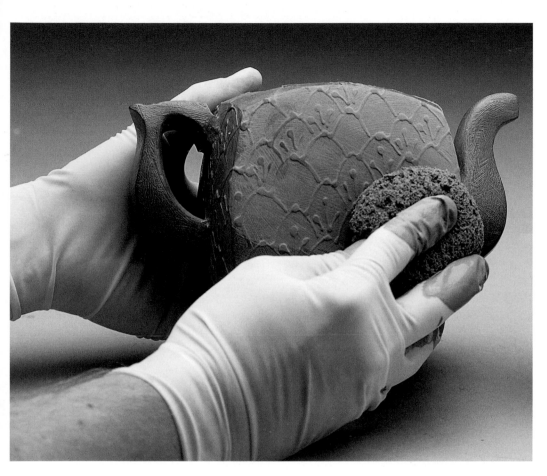

The pot is bisque-fired, then glazed inside. The outside is coated with what Pinnell calls a "patina," which is a simple mixture of one part metal oxide (in this case a mixture of titanium dioxide and cobalt oxide) to two parts gerstley borate. This is combined with water and a thin layer is applied to the surface of the teapot with a sponge. After the patina coating has dried completely, it is wiped off of the raised details using a dry, clean cloth.

 The finished pot, with glazed interior and patina surface on exterior, is fired to cone 04 in an electric kiln, then "soaks" in the kiln (which means holding that temperature) for sixty minutes. The kiln is cooled very slowly—about one hundred degrees the first hour. The slow cooling encourages the patina to take on a matte, metallic surface. If cooled too quickly, the surface would appear more glossy.

Notes from the Studio

After much trial and error, research and experimentation, Pinnell has arrived at the following methods to ensure consistent results when using terra sigillata.

> Terra sigillata is a thin, deflocculated clay slip that produces a smooth, tight skin on the surface of the pot. It is made by mixing dry clay, water, and deflocculant, stirring well, and allowing the mixture to settle. This will separate the coarse particles of clay, which settle out, from the finer particles, which stay in suspension longer.

> Terra sigillata may be used alone, or it may be combined with oxides or stains to produce a variety of colors. The proportion of clay to water, and the length of time the mixture is allowed to settle, can vary.

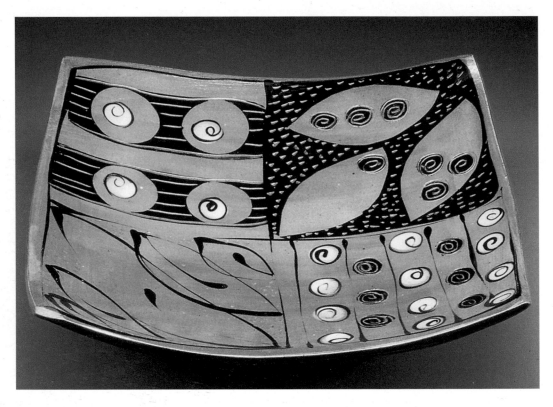

∧ *Raised Square Platter*

by SUZE LINDSAY

Salt-fired stoneware with slip decoration
3" x 18" x 18" (8 cm x 46 cm x 46 cm)

∧ *Sectional Urn*

by STEVEN HILL

Single-fired stoneware
21" x 21" (53 cm x 53 cm)

Spring in Mardi Gras Teapot **>**

by LINDA ARBUCKLE
Majolica on terra-cotta
13" x 10" x 4" (33 cm x 25 cm x 10 cm)

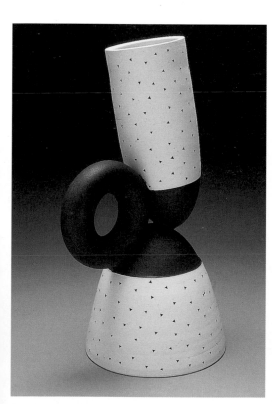

∧ *Cup*

by JOSEPH MOLINARO
Porcelain, fired to cone 8 oxidation, with
black glaze
18" x 8" x 6" (46 cm x 20 cm x 15 cm)

v *Margarita Pitcher and Tumblers*

by SUZE LINDSAY

Salt-fired stoneware with slip decoration
18" x 9" x 4.5" (46 cm x 23 cm x 11 cm)

^ *Pitcher*

by JOSEPH MOLINARO

Porcelain, fired to cone 8 in oxidation, with black glaze and crackle slip
16" x 8" x 6" (41 cm x 20 cm x 15 cm)

< *Teapot*

by PETER PINNELL

Low-fired, with terra sigillata and patina surface
4" x 6" x 5" (10 cm x 15 cm x 13 cm)

∨ *Cypress Ewer*

by STEVEN HILL

Stoneware, wheel thrown and altered, single-fired
17" x 11" (43 cm x 28 cm)

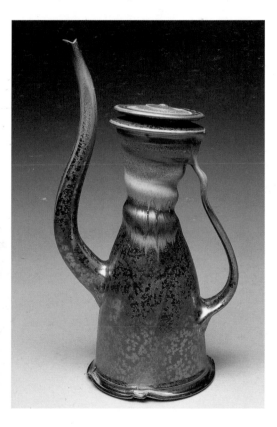

< *Platter*

by STEVEN HILL

Single-fired, stoneware
21" (53 cm) diameter

∧ *Teapot*

by PETER PINNELL

Low-fired, with terra sigillata and patina surface
4" x 6" x 5" (10 cm x 15 cm x 13 cm)

∨ *Shape of Spring Teapot*

by LINDA ARBUCKLE

Majolica on terra-cotta
6" wide x 13" tall x 10" long (33 cm x 25 cm x 15 cm)

< *Oval Footed Platter with Lateral Leaves*

by LINDA ARBUCKLE

Majolica on terra-cotta
8" wide x 3.5" high x 20" long (9 cm x 51 cm x 20 cm)

v *Gloriosa Teapot*

by L1NDA ARBUCKLE

Majolica on terra-cotta
6" wide x 12.5" tall x 9.5" long (32 cm x 24 cm x 15 cm)

< *Tureen & Plate*

by STANLEY MACE ANDERSEN

Earthenware with majolica decoration
10.5" tall x 12" diameter (27 cm x 30 cm)

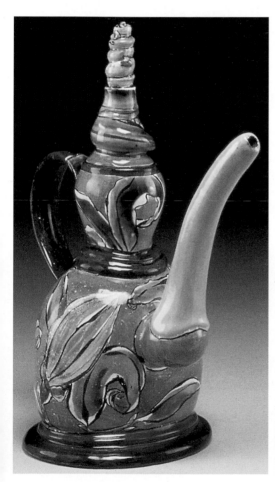

> *Wall Platter*

by STANLEY MACE ANDERSEN

Earthenware with majolica decoration
20" (51 cm) diameter

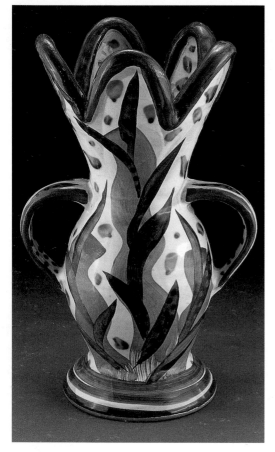

^ *Vase*

by STANLEY MACE ANDERSEN

Earthenware with majolica decoration
14" tall x 7" diameter (36 cm x 18 cm)

> *Tripoidal Lidded Cauldron*

by ELEANORA EDEN

Polychrome white earthenware
9" tall x 10" diameter (23 cm x 25 cm)

< *Footed Boat: Wisteria*

by LINDA ARBUCKLE

Majolica on terra-cotta
19" long x 9" wide x 5.5" high (48 cm x 23 cm x 14 cm)

∧ *Lidded Ewer*

by ELEANORA EDEN

Polychrome white earthenware
10" tall x 7" long x 5" wide (25 cm x 18 cm x 13 cm)

< *Biscuit Jar: Plenty*

by LINDA ARBUCKLE

Majolica on terra-cotta
13" high x 10.5" diameter (33 cm x 27 cm)

FIRING

Copper Green Carved, Lidded Jar

by JIM CONNELL
Raku
16" x 16" x 16" (41 cm x 41 cm x 41 cm)

F1R1NG

The history of ceramics tells the story of our growing understanding and control of fire. From the ancient practice of firing pots in open-air fires to computerized, programmable electric kilns, potters choose the approach and equipment that best suits their attitudes, their work, and their environment. A young potter working in an academic environment may be limited by the school's equipment. An urban potter may long to fire his or her work in a wood kiln, but cannot because of space limitations or problems with access to fuel. City ordinances may also be restrictive as, almost certainly, are environmental guidelines.

A potter would be wise to consider his or her own personality and temperament when choosing a method of firing. Some potters may need more control over the outcome of their firings and opt for the reliability of an electric kiln. Other potters may enjoy the uncertainty of an anagama or raku firing. The odd "happy accident" can remind us that the hand of Nature is often more expressive than our own. It can reveal the unexpected beauty of a flame path captured in a carbon-trap glaze, or the elegant drip of ash frozen on the side of an anagama pot. Potters, including Jim Connell, have adapted their approach in an effort to balance some control with the happy accidents that can be achieved in raku.

The final consideration when choosing a method of firing is the work itself. What do you want it to look like? The translucent elegance of porcelain may require a high-temperature gas kiln. A rainbow of colors can be achieved in an electric kiln fired to low temperatures. A wood-fired kiln, such as the one Linda Christianson uses, can produce an earthy, understated surface on the ware. In the end, fluency is a potter's best option. Experimenting with a variety of approaches will lead to the best choice for you—and your work.

Faceted Jar

by MALCOLM DAVIS

Porcelain, fired in gas reduction kiln
10" tall x 6" diameter
(25 cm x 15 cm)

Bottle

by DAVIE MARIE RENEAU

Porcelain, fired in anagama kiln
8" (20 cm) tall

Copper Green Carved Vase

by JIM CONNELL

Raku-fired
7" tall (18 cm)

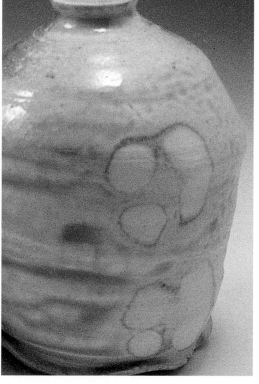

"By relinquishing some of the control over the finished surface to the firing process, 1 allow the reduction chamber to become the final decorator."

—Jim Connell

RAKU FIRING IN ELECTRIC KILNS

Perhaps more than any other process in ceramics, raku, the ancient technique of fast-firing and pulling pottery red-hot from the kiln, is rich in tradition and superstition, and rules. Jim Connell is one artist who has had the courage to question the rules of raku. When he was a graduate student at the University of Illinois, he knew the rules. But one weekend, he happened on another student firing raku ware in an electric kiln. Connell argued with the young man, running through all the reasons he knew why it was a bad idea. "You'll get shocked! You'll ruin the elements in the kiln!!" But the other student was unmoved. When it was over, the student was healthy, the kiln was undamaged, and the work looked good.

Connell was forced to recall this event five years later, when he was teaching at Winthrop University in Rock Hill South Carolina. An impending renovation meant there was no working gas kiln and no means of getting one for some time. Still desiring to use reduction, and thinking back to the unsanctioned electric raku firing he had witnessed in graduate school, he decided to try it himself. As a result, Connell has been able to achieve, over the past several years, beautiful and reliable work using electric kilns, all the while debunking the rules about raku—rules that, for the most part, turned out to be myths.

SETTING UP:
Making a Faceted Raku Jar

To make his distinctive covered jars, Connell uses raku clay, which is more porous than standard low-fire or stoneware clay. Grog or sand is added to the clay to increase its porosity, allowing the pot to survive the rapid changes in temperature without "dunting," or cracking.

Connell starts by throwing a jar with fairly thick walls. The seat, or mouth opening, is measured and a lid is thrown to the proper size. After the clay wall of the pot has dried and stiffened slightly, Connell facets the form using a length of wire. He cuts down through the thickness of the wall at angles to achieve the twisted facets on the form.

Tools

- raku tongs

- gloves

- safety glasses

- metal garbage can with lid

- torn newspaper

The process starts with the application of a healthy coat of raku glaze to the pot. Connell sprays the glaze on, but it can also be dipped or brushed on. The pots are dry-footed (wiped clean on the bottom) and loaded into an electric kiln.

The pots are fired at least twice. Initially, the pots are fired to cone 08 and allowed to cool slowly in the kiln. They are not "pulled" or reduced during this first firing. This first step in the process allows Connell to correct two common problems: pinholing and inadequate glaze application.

More glaze is added to the piece after the first firing to correct any problems, and it is then reloaded into the (cooled) electric kiln. By never placing cold pieces into hot kilns, Connell has significantly reduced the amount of breakage in his work. Notice the dry glaze that was added after the first firing to correct pinholing and thin spots.

When the kiln reaches cone 08, the lid is opened (or in this case, removed) and the red-hot pot is removed with long metal tongs. It is quickly, but gently, placed in the metal "reduction" can, which has been filled with torn newspaper. The heat of the pot ignites the paper. Here, the paper is already burning because the jar's small lid was placed in the reduction can moments earlier. The can is covered to suffocate the flames and allowed to smoke for a few minutes.

After being covered for two or three minutes, the can is opened briefly to "burp," which allows the pot to reoxidize slightly. Because some surfaces of the pot may be covered by the paper on which they rest, the pot may reoxidize unevenly, resulting in a more interesting surface. As oxygen enters the can, the paper inside reignites. The lid is quickly replaced, and the pot remains in the reduction can for several hours, until it is cool to the touch. "It is hard not to peek," Connell says. "But if you can walk away and come back in a couple of hours, you will fare better in the long run."

After cooling, the pot is revealed in the reduction can. Pots are finally scrubbed with steel wool and cleanser and examined for any imperfections. Depending on how Connell evaluates the results, he may refire a pot several times, sometimes adding more glaze, and always reducing it. He never "freezes" the surface of the pot by dunking it or spraying it with water while the pot is very hot, as is the common practice in raku firings. Doing so greatly increases the likelihood that the pot will crack from the thermal shock.

Notes from the Studio

Connell uses these techniques to achieve work that combines the beauty of raku surfaces and the consistency of a controlled firing process.

> A glaze goes through a series of changes as it increases in temperature: drying, cracking, bubbling (gas release), and settling. In a normal gas raku firing, this process is rushed through in as little as fifteen minutes. If the firing cycle is extended to six to eight hours, there is adequate time for the glaze to melt and settle.

> Various materials can be used in the reduction can to produce textures. Pine needles, sawdust, and leaves produce a rough surface because the glaze is still soft when it is first placed onto the combustible material.

Connell uses newspaper because it is readily available, burns quickly, and does not produce a rough surface.

> Connell relies on pyrometric cones (cone 08) for the final firing. This is a break from the common raku practice of watching the glaze for visual signs of melting and then pulling the pot from the heat. Says Connell: "Cones allow me the most even, consistent firings from load to load. The glaze may be melted at cone 010, but it won't look as good as it will when it's fired to cone 08."

"The atmospheric changes that occur in a wood kiln produce spotting and blushing on the pots. A tiny bit of salt thrown in adds a slight sheen in some areas. After some twenty years of firing with wood, 1 still love that surface and enjoy the physicality of the process."

—Linda Christianson

WOOD FIRING

Leave Minneapolis heading northeast and you'll soon find yourself in rolling farmland nestled between the upper Mississippi and the St. Croix rivers. If someone has drawn you a map, you might find yourself driving down a long farm road outside Lindstrom, Minnesota. Turn into the right driveway and you'll be at Linda Christianson's home and pottery.

A kiln shed sits in the front yard, and on the front porch pots are arranged on benches, shelves, and a few small tables. The porch is the pottery showroom. Subtle and quiet, these pots seem a logical part of this harsh but beautiful environment. They are simple in form and decoration, requiring some time and attention on the part of the viewer to reveal their real beauty. They echo the colors of old snow or split pine, sometimes with a touch of a light sage green. If no one is home, you can add up your purchases, wrap your pots, leave your money, and take your change.

Open and friendly, Christianson displays an abundance of dry Minnesotan humor, all qualities that are recognizable in her work. Fired in a two-chamber wood kiln, her pots are often left at least partially unglazed, yet they function well for preparing and serving food. The forms are useful but also playful and animated.

GETTING READY TO FIRE:
Loading and Firing the Wood Kiln

Because of the weather extremes in Minnesota, Christianson often hangs a tarp over the area surrounding the kiln shed. It keeps her warm in winter and shades her from the sun in the summer. The shed has no walls so that the smoke created during the firing can be vented from the area. The roof over the kiln protects it from rain and snow.

Christianson separates the wood into three types: wood cut to the length of the firebox; scraps (left over from cutting the firebox wood); and longer, thinner pieces used to "side stoke." After the wood is prepared, Christianson mixes "wadding," which is material used to elevate pots from the shelves and from other pots to prevent them from fusing together during the firing.

Tools

- ax

- pyrometric cones

- wheelbarrow

- draw rings

- gloves

- kneeling pad

- long metal rods for stirring coals and pulling draw rings

Ware to be fired sits near the kiln, sorted by size and shape. Loading the kiln takes time, patience, and a lot of planning. Pots of similar size and shape can be loaded lip to lip (with wadding in between). Christianson tries to use the space in the ware chambers as economically as possible. In effect, loading is like trying to solve a large, three-dimensional puzzle.

Christianson's kiln has two ware chambers and two main fire boxes (also called "bourry" boxes). Here, the first chamber is being loaded with ware. Plates are loaded upside-down. They are wadded, stacked, and often suspended over another pot to keep the plate's lip off the shelf. Christianson loads according to the way the kiln fires. For example, she loads work glazed with lower-temperature glazes in areas of the kiln that typically fire cooler.

After loading the kiln, Christianson starts a small fire in the main fire boxes, using charcoal, coal, and large hardwood logs. This fire will preheat the kiln overnight. It is important to start slowly; a wood fire can get *very* hot very fast, which could easily crack the ware. The next morning, she feeds the fire with scraps of wood much shorter than the length of the fireboxes. Usually, she can get close to bisque temperatures (around 1,800 degrees Fahrenheit) using just these scraps.

As the kiln approaches bisque temperature, Christianson switches to the larger wood, which is stoked into both bourry boxes. She likes the bourry-box design because it is cooler to stoke and easier on the eyes in terms of the brightness of the fire. Its disadvantage is that all the wood must be cut to one length, to fall flat on the hobs.

As the temperature in the kiln rises, Christianson moves to side-stoking the main chamber, which helps the floor area and the back of the ware chamber to get hot. When the first chamber is nearly at temperature, she begins side-stoking the second chamber. The wood lands on grates and gets "super-heated" air from the first chamber. The pace of the firing is now hectic. As the first chamber reaches temperature, salt is added through the stoke hole and more wood is stoked on top of the salt. The fire in the main fire boxes must also be maintained. When the first chamber is finished, stoking in the second chamber increases.

When the second chamber reaches temperature, all stoke holes are closed, the damper in the chimney is closed, and the kiln is allowed to cool. During the cooling phase, the kiln shed is cleaned and organized, wood is restacked, and the area is prepared for unloading the pots. Finally, after two days of cooling, the bricks of the door are pulled down to reveal the finished ware.

As the kiln is unloaded, pots are cleaned, inspected, and the wads are knocked off. This area, at the top of the first chamber, near the back, shows the effects of the light salting. A slight sheen is apparent on the surface of the ware.

Notes from the Studio

Over the years, Linda Christianson has developed these useful methods for wood firing.

> Christianson's recipe for wadding is (by volume) one part Edgar plastic kaolin, one part alumina hydrate. Mix dry, add water slowly, and mix until it reaches a soft clay-like consistency. During the winter, keep the wadding warm enough to be pliable to prevent it from freezing while the kiln is being loaded.

> It is vitally important that enough wood has been cut, sorted, stacked, and dried before the kiln is loaded. The worst-case scenario is running out of wood before the kiln reaches temperature. It is nearly impossible to fire successfully if you have to cut or sort wood while stoking.

All pottery produced in the village is fired in open fires, but the approach to the firing varies with the size and shape of each pot.

POTTERS OF JATUN MOLINO

Deep in the rainforest of Ecuador is the tiny, remote village of Jatun Molino, or "big whirlpool," a feature of the river, the Rio Bobanaza, near the village. The village houses approximately 100 people. The inhabitants work communally, fulfilling the needs of the entire village. Men and women have distinct roles and tasks to perform, and the children grow up understanding their place in the community.

The men hunt, build and repair huts, and weave baskets. The women gather and prepare food, and make pottery. Children participate in these activities, working with the adults and learning the skills that have been handed down for generations.

Most of the women potters work in their homes, creating pottery for practical daily use, including vessels for eating, drinking, cooking, and storage. The women also make *chicha* jars, which hold the main beverage produced and consumed by the villagers. *Chicha* is made from yucca root, which is mashed and then chewed. After chewing the root, the women spit the liquid into large common vessels where it ferments into a strong alcoholic drink. The jars for fermenting and storing *chicha* vary in shape and decoration, but are generally large, averaging two to three feet (.6 to .9 meter) in height. All pottery produced in the village is fired in open fires, but the approach to the firing varies with the size and shape of each pot.

Firing the Chicha Jars

Chicha Jar
36" tall x 26" diameter (91 cm x 66 cm)

◎ Large jars in which *chicha* is fermenting. The slightly pointed bottoms of the jars are buried in the sand to keep the jars stable and to help the *chicha* cool. The leaves on the top keep insects out and aid in the fermentation.

◎ Neba, a fourteen-year-old girl in the village, prepares to fire a large *chicha* jar. The jar is first suspended upside-down on a frame-work of "green," or freshly cut, sticks. The mouth of the jar, now nearest the ground, is held about 2" to 3" (5 to 8 cm) above the ground by the supporting framework. A very small, simmering fire is started directly below the mouth of the jar to slowly heat the interior. In this way, the vessel acts as its own kiln.

⊚ Dry wood is then stacked around the bulk of the large jar.

⊚ Neba fans the small fire below the mouth of the jar to ignite the dry wood stacked around the pot.

⊚ Once ignited, the dry wood on the exterior of the pot burns itself out in approximately fifteen to twenty minutes. The pot then cools for up to one hour before it is handled. If any cracking occurs during the firing, the women patch the pots with sap from the *Chillquillo* tree. This sap, white when applied, darkens and hardens to a tar-like density when it is heated.

Firing the Mucauas

In addition to creating the large *chicha* jars, the women of the village make a variety of other forms. A common vessel in their homes is a small bowl, or *mucaua*, which is used for both drinking the *chicha* and for eating food.

Mucaua
Approximately 7" (18 cm) diameter

🌀 These pots and other smaller vessels are often highly decorated with colored slips applied with delicate brushes made of human hair. Because the *mucauas* are small and concave in shape, the women fire them in succession on small fires right inside their huts.

🌀 The women's approach to firing the *mucauas* is simple, yet ingenious. The pot is inverted and set into a slightly larger bowl, which has already been hardened by fire and in which a large hole has been made in the bottom.

The two bowls are placed onto a small, smoldering fire. The heat from the coals enters through the hole in the bottom bowl and warms the top, inverted *mucaua* from within.

The *mucaua* is covered with a thick layer of hot ash to insulate it. After being covered, it is allowed to heat slowly on the fire for a few minutes. (Notice the pieces of clay set near the fire to dry.)

⊚ More wood is added to the fire to reach higher temperatures. The fire is maintained for a few minutes more and then allowed to return to smoldering.

⊚ The *mucaua* and the firing bowl it is held in are removed from the fire with sticks or machetes. The firing bowl is used as a support for the newly fired *mucaua* while the potter rubs sap over its interior. This sap acts as a protective coating in lieu of a glaze.

The potter turns the *mucaua* over to cover the exterior with the protective sap (a chunk of which she holds in her mouth). Notice the hole in the bottom of the supporting bowl.

The sap of the *Chillquillo* tree is applied while the *mucaua* is still warm, to enhance the decoration and to make the bowl watertight.

∧ *Vase*

by LINDA CHRISTIANSON

Stoneware, fired in wood kiln
7" high x 6" wide x 4" diameter (18 cm x 15 cm x 10 cm)

∨ *Copper Green Carved Pitcher*

by JIM CONNELL

Raku-fired
17" tall (43 cm)

< *Teapot with Feet*

by MALCOLM DAVIS

Porcelain, fired in gas reduction kiln
10" tall x 7" wide x 6" deep (25 cm x 18 cm x 15 cm)

∧ *Oil Cans*

by LINDA CHRISTIANSON

Wood-fired stoneware
Ranging in height up to 7" (18 cm)

∧ *Five Square Plates*

by LINDA CHRISTIANSON

Wood-fired stoneware
8" x 8" x 1.5" (20 cm x 20 cm x 4 cm)

∧ *Shino Tea Bowl*

by MALCOLM DAVIS

Porcelain, fired in gas reduction kiln
3.5" tall (9 cm)

∧ *Juri-Juri Figurative Vessel*

by the POTTERS OF JATUN MOLINO

Hand built from indigenous clay and decorated with colored slips.

∧ *Faceted Jar*

by MALCOLM DAVIS

Porcelain, fired in gas reduction kiln
10" tall x 6" diameter (25 cm x 15 cm)

< *Lidded Copper Green Carved Jar (detail)*

by **JIM CONNELL**

∧ *Copper Green Carved, Lidded Jar*

by **JIM CONNELL**

Raku, fired in electric kiln
16" x 16" (41 cm x 41 cm)

∧ *Copper Green Carved Vase*

by **JIM CONNELL**

Raku-fired
7" tall (18 cm)

∧ *Copper Green Carved, Lidded Jar*

by **JIM CONNELL**

Raku
16" x 16" x 16" (41 cm x 41 cm x 41 cm)

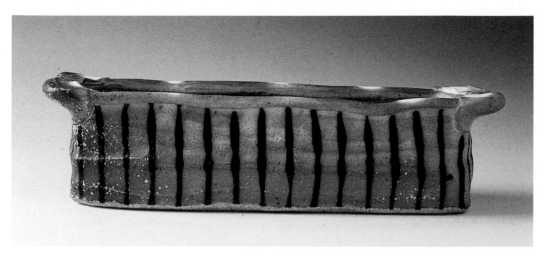

< *Oval Baker*

by L1NDA CHR1ST1ANSON

Wood-fired stoneware
4" x 14" x 6" (10 cm x 36 cm x 15 cm)

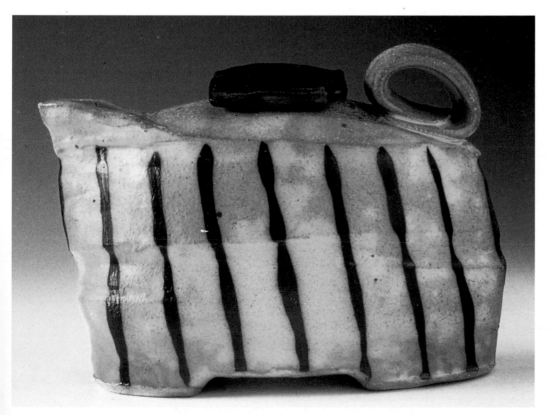

∧ *Pitcher*

by L1NDA CHR1ST1ANSON

Stoneware, fired in wood kiln
10" high x 9" wide x 5" diameter (25 cm x 23 cm x 13 cm)

∧ *Teapot*

by L1NDA CHR1ST1ANSON

Stoneware, fired in wood kiln
8" high x 11" wide x 7" diameter (20 cm x 28 cm x 18 cm)

∨ *Three Bottles*

by DAVIE MARIE RENEAU

Porcelain, fired in anagama kiln
Tallest: 9" tall (23 cm)

∧ *Copper Green Carved Vase*

by JIM CONNELL

Raku-fired
13" tall (33 cm)

∧ *Pitcher*

by DAVIE MARIE RENEAU
Stoneware, fired in anagama kiln
10" tall (25 cm)

RECIPES

> *Wall Platter*

by STANLEY MACE ANDERSEN

Earthenware with majolica decoration
20" (51 cm) diameter

Recipes

If your house caught fire and all living creatures had been brought out safely, what might tempt you to run back in? The family photos? I believe most potters would run back to save their glaze and clay recipes. A potter's collection of favorite recipes is a treasure. Some keep copies in a safe-deposit box. Others keep copies in a variety of places for safety and convenience.

Many potters never reveal their favorite recipes to other potters. Others share information freely, believing that no one else can ever *really* duplicate a glaze exactly. The artists in *Creative Pottery* have been generous enough to share their favorite clay and glaze recipes. Of course, owning someone's recipe is no guarantee that you can duplicate the look of his or her surfaces; clays and glazes are affected by mixing, application, and firing techniques. But it is a place to start when pursuing a particular surface for your own work. The clay and glaze products listed here are available in the United States, and it is fairly easy to find the equivalent products in other countries. If some of the brand names are unavailable in your area, contact your local pottery supplier who can recommend alternative products.

There is an old story out of Alfred University, in New York, about a student who developed a beautiful plum-colored glaze. The other students asked for the recipe, but he would share it with no one. The students knew the recipe was locked up in his locker. One night, after the student went home, the other students removed the hinges from the locker door and took the recipe. They returned the notebook and replaced the hinges. Then they mixed a barrel of the glaze and covered an entire kiln load of work in it. When the kiln was unloaded, the student who owned the recipe was shocked. He asked to see the others' recipes. No one would share it with him.

RECIPE SAMPLER

Arbuckle Terra-Cotta Clay Cone 08 to 03

Red art clay	50.0 pounds
XX saggar	20.0
Fireclay	20.0
Flint	12.0
Talc	5.0
Spodumene	3.0
Nepheline syenite	5.0
Very fine grog	2.0-8.0
Barium carbonate	0.5

Note: Barium is needed to prevent scumming.

Note:

The clay and glaze products listed in the recipes are available in the United States, and it is fairly easy to find the equivalent products in other countries. If some of the brand names are unavailable in your area, contact your local pottery supplier who can recommend alternative products.

Linda Arbuckle

Majolica Base (Opaque White)

	Cone 03	Cone 05
Frit 3124	65.75 grams	58.00 gr
F-4 soda feldspar	17.24	20.00
Avery kaolin or EPK	10.82	2.00
Nepheline syenite	6.24	7.00
Add:		
Tin oxide	5.00	5.00
Zircopax	10.00	10.00
Bentonite	2.00	2.00

Black Oxide Mix for Overglaze Decoration

Black iron oxide............................20.00 grams

Cobalt carbonate............................15.00

Manganese dioxide....................20.0

Black chrome.................................5.0

Shiny Clear
Cone 06 to 04

Gerstley borate............................55.00 grams

EPK...30.00

Flint...15.00

Note: This glaze can be brushed on, or you can thin it with water to dip ware.

Majolica Colorants for Overglaze Decoration

1 part (by volume) oxide to
1 part gerstley borate:

Copper carbonate	for	Blue green
Iron oxide	for	Brown
Cobalt carbonate	for	Blue

1 part (by volume) oxide to
3 to 4 parts gerstley borate:

Chrome	for	Opaque green
Rutile	for	Rusty orange
Mason stains	for	Variety of Colors

Note: Mason Stains

- *"Body" stains, such as Mason 6020 pink, titanium yellow, and lavender, are too refractory and will leave a "pigskinned" surface.*
- *Many blue Mason stains are somewhat refractory, as well. Mix them with 4 parts gerstley borate.*
- *Many lovely yellow stains contain lead! Be sure to read the ingredients.*

Pale Green Liner
Cone 8 to 9

Potash feldspar.................27.30 grams

Whiting..............................19.65

EPK...................................20.05

Flint..................................33.00

Add:
Red iron oxide....................1.00

Note: For a darker green, increase the red iron oxide up to 3%.

Linda Christianson

#6 Tile Slip
Cone 6 to 10

#6 tile clay........................100 grams

Bentonite.............................2

Black Decorating
Slip
Cone 6 to 10

Note: Christianson uses a commercial produc
straight from the jar: Duncan Easy Stroke #013
(Cobalt Jet Black Underglaze)

Clay Recipe for Wood-Salt
Cone 8 to 10

AP green fireclay.............40.0 pounds

Helmar kaolin...................30.0

Custer feldspar.................24.0

OM4 ball clay...................16.0

Pine Lake fireclay.............10.0

Flint.....................................9.0

Sand....................................7.0

Pyropholite.........................6.8

Grog....................................6.5

Red Shino
Cone 9 to 10

Nepheline syenite........4500 grams

F-4 soda feldspar..........1080

OM4 ball clay...............1520

EPK.................................2000

Soda ash.......................1900

Add:
Red art clay...................660

Note: This glaze works best in heavy reduction.

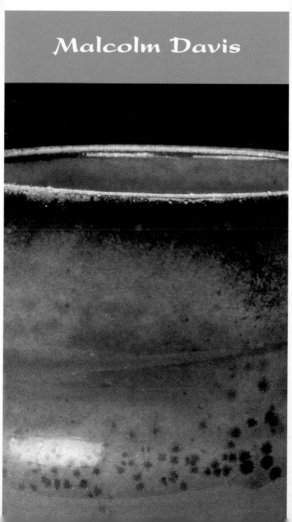

Malcolm Davis

Raku Clay Body
Cone 010 to 04

Hawthorn Bond
fireclay...................................50 pounds

AP green fireclay...............50

OM4 ball clay....................25

Foundry Hill Creme...........25

Grog or sand.....................10

Kyanite.............................15

Jim Connell

Ferguson Blue
Raku Glaze
Cone 06

Frit 3110.........................700 grams

Colemanite (or G.B.).........50

Flint.................................100

Soda ash.........................100

EPK.................................50

Add:

Copper carbonate............30

White Crackle Raku Glaze Cone 06

Colemanite......................400 grams

Frit 3110...........................400

Nepheline syenite...........200

Note: Gerstley borate can be substituted for colemanite, as needed.

Higby Copper Green Raku Glaze Cone 06

Frit 3110...........................700 grams

Colemanite......................50

Flint.................................120

Soda ash..........................50

EPK.................................50

Add:

Copper carbonate...........80

Red iron oxide.................10

White Stoneware Clay for Single Firing Cone 8 to 10

KT 1-4 ball clay...........100 pounds........(35%)

Hawthorn Bond fireclay.......................50.....................(17.5)

OM4 ball clay..............50.....................(17.5)

Custer potash feldspar........................20.....................(7.0)

200-mesh flint..............27.....................(9.5)

35-mesh flint grog.......38.....................(13.3)

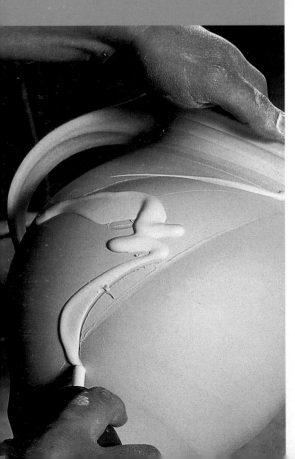

Steven Hill

Note:

35-mesh flint grog is actually a fireclay grog. It has a light gray color and is relatively fine.

SH Copper Wash for Raw Glazing Cone 8 to 10

F-4 soda feldspar..............18 grams

Dolomite............................10

Whiting..............................90

Kaolin................................70

Flint...................................36

Add:

Bentonite...........................6

Copper carbonate...........14

SNGN Stony Yellow Glaze for Raw Glazing Cone 8 to 10

F-4 soda feldspar..............33.5 grams

Kaolin................................ 25.0

Dolomite............................17.0

Talc....................................10.5

Spodumene........................7.0

Whiting................................4.5

Add:

Bentonite............................2.0

Red iron oxide....................1.9

Note:

For Stony Blue Glaze, lower the amount of red iron oxide to .85 and add .9 grams of cobalt carbonate.

SH Copper Wash Cone 8 to 10

Nepheline syenite...........110 grams

Gerstley borate................24

Whiting..............................22

Flint....................................64

Add:

Bentonite............................8

Copper carbonate.............10

Tin oxide............................20

Basic
Terra Sigillata

By weight, mix one part dry clay of choice to two parts water. (Remember: 1 pint water equals 1 pound.)

Add: Sodium silicate: .25% to .50% of the dry weight of the clay. Stir well and allow to settle.

Note: Less plastic clays (such as red art and fireclay) will settle in 6 to 8 hours. More plastic clays (such as ball clay) may take 24 to 48 hours to settle. Choose the clay based on its color and temperature.

Peter Pinnell

Pete's E-3
Clear Glaze
Cone 04

Frit 3124.............................70 grams

Strontium carbonate........10

Kaolin.................................10

Nepheline syenite............10

Add:

Bentonite.............................2

Note: Add muriatic acid or Epsom salts to prevent settling. Like all frit glazes, it should be applied fairly thinly to avoid cloudiness.

Rosie's Base Glaze
Cone 04

Gerstley borate.................50 grams

Plastic vitrox.....................40

Flint.................................10

Note: To alter the color of either preceding glaze, add up to 10% Mason stain.

Darby's Satin Semi-Gloss
Cone 04

Spodumene.........................50 grams

Gerstley borate....................30

Flint.................................20

Add:

Bentonite................................2

Mason stain...........................1% to 10%
(#6600 makes a semi-gloss black liner glaze.)

Pete's Shiny Black Glaze
Cone 04

Frit 3124.............................45 grams

Frit 3289.............................45

Kaolin.................................10

Add:

Bentonite.............................2

Mason stain #6600
(black)................................10

Note: Add Epsom salts or muriatic acid to prevent settling.

Michael's Clay Body for Salt Firing
Cone 7 to 10

AP green fireclay.............70 pounds

#6 tile clay.........................20

Ball clay.............................10

Fine grog............................12

Potash feldspar.................9

Michael Simon

Rob's Copper Green
Cone 8 to 10

Cornwall stone.................63.5 grams

Whiting...............................15.2

Gerstley borate.................4.3

Bentonite............................3.0

Add:

Copper carbonate.............8.5

Ruggles and Rankin White Slip
Cone 8 to 10

Silica...........................1 part

Potash feldspar.................1 part

Ball clay.......................1 part

Avery kaolin....................1 part

Add:

Bentonite, a "smidge" (equal to approximately 3%)

Note:

EPK or another kaolin may be substituted for Avery, if unavailable.

Black Slip Glaze
Cone 8 to 10

Albany slip.....................90 grams

Nepheline syenite..............5

Add:

Cobalt oxide....................5

Note: Alberta slip or synthetic Albany slip may be substituted.

EPK Throwing Body
Cone 8 to 10

#6 tile clay	20 pounds
EPK	35
Flint	10
Pyrax	10
Custer feldspar	20
XX saggar	10
Bentonite	2
Macaloid	2

Note:

This body flashes orange in a wood kiln.

Black Clay Body
Cone 8 to 10

Ocmulgee clay	100 pounds
Ball clay	20
Goldart	30
Hawthorn Bond fireclay	20
Red art clay	16
Barnard clay	10
Grog	10

Add:

Red iron oxide	4

Chris Staley

Staley Ice Blue Glaze (Variation 1)
Cone 8 to 10

very kaolin	935 grams
Whiting	1869
Custer potash feldspar	2804
flint	3738

Add:

Zircopax	467
Bentonite	187

Rutile Slip
Cone 9 to 10

Potash feldspar	2.00 pounds
Talc	2.00
Ball clay	4.00
EPK	6.00
Silica	5.00

Add:

Rutile	2.85
Bentonite	0.50

Pier Black Glaze
Cone 9 to 10

Custer potash feldspar	432 grams
EPK	240
Dolomite	240
Whiting	48
Borax	55
Iron chromate	67
Cobalt carbonate	67

Conrad's Altered Engobe for Green or Bisqued Pieces Cone 04 to 8

Borax or soda ash...............5 grams

Custer potash feldspar...............................15

Whiting.................................5

Kaolin..................................20

Nepheline syenite.............10

Kentucky ball clay.............20

Silica...................................25

Add:

Mason stain #6600 (black)..................................12

Note:

For an added sheen at cone 6, add 20% extra nepheline syenite.

Lana Wilson

Lana's Red #88 Glaze Cone 06

Red art clay.......................88 grams

Frit 3134..............................12

Note: Lana uses this glaze after a piece has been fired to cone 6 with Conrad's Altered Engobe.

Lana's Purple Aqua Glaze
Cone 06 to 6

Nepheline syenite............45 grams

Barium carbonate............45

Frit 626 or Frit 3289.............4

Bentonite............................2

Add:

Copper carbonate........4–10

Note:

Apply a little thicker than milk. It will be blue/purple where thin; aqua where thicker.

Dry Borax Engobe
Cone 06 to 6

Borax.................................14 grams

Edgar Plastic Kaolin
(EPK)..................................57

Silica..................................29

Note: Use under Wilson's Purple Aqua or any plain glaze.

Tools

It is often said that a potter's most important tools are the hands, the heart, and the head, and the making of pottery requires little more. But as potters refine the craft and expand it into new visions of what clay can be, the collection of tools used to make pottery is also expanded and refined.

It can be problematic that a very small number of companies produce most of the basic tools that potters use. Students are trained using the exact tools their teachers were trained with, and will probably teach others using the same tools from the same company. Yet, potters strive to make their own pots unique.

Some potters choose to make some of their own tools, designed for specific tasks in the creation of their work. Chris Staley uses handmade metal ribs of his own design, shapes his own wooden modeling tools, and stretches springs to use as cut-off wires. Others take another creative approach—utilizing objects or tools designed for other purposes. Lana Wilson uses a pastry dough roller when joining slabs of clay. Steven Hill uses an enema syringe for slip-trailing. Kitchen and hardware stores, even toy stores, can be a source of useful studio tools.

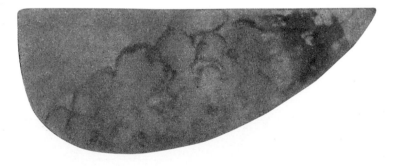

Potters can be as protective of their tools as they are of their recipes. Some potters, when they travel to workshops, carry their tools with them on the plane. If luggage is lost or delayed, they can still give the workshop. And it is easier to replace clothing than a favorite tool that works in harmony with the hand.

I have owned a particular wooden rib for more than fifteen years. It has warped over time to fit my hand perfectly. I know its curve instinctively. We work together like an old vaudeville act. I could never really replace it and would be lost without it. But I *am* conscious of my dependency on this particular tool.

Sometimes it is prudent to stop and consider the tool in your hand. Is it *really* doing the job you want? Or have you adjusted your expectations of the pot to the limits of the tools you use? Like many things that we grow to depend on in our life, tools can be useful servants or cruel masters.

Where To Learn More

Pottery courses are taught at most colleges and universities. Many schools offer noncredit or community education courses in addition to credit courses. The following are some of the better schools that offer "intensive" workshops in pottery, where instructors are often recruited to teach classes from one to eight weeks.

United States

California

Idyllwild Arts Summer Program
P.O. Box 38
Idyllwild, CA 92549
Phone: (909) 659-2171 ext. 365
Fax: (909) 659-5463

Mendocino Art Center
P.O. Box 765
Mendocino, CA 95460
Phone: (707) 937-5818

Colorado

Anderson Ranch Arts Center
P.O. Box 5598
Snowmass Village, CO 81615
Phone: (970) 923-3181
Fax: (970) 923-3871

Arvada Center for the Arts and Humanities
6901 Wadsworth Boulevard
Arvada, CO 80003
Phone: (303) 431-3080 ext. 3109

Illinois

Native Soil
602 Davis Street
Evanston, IL 60201
Phone: (847) 733-8006
Fax: (847) 733-8042

Maine

Haystack Mountain School of Crafts
P.O. Box 518
Deer Isle, ME 04627
Phone: (207) 348-2306

Watershed Center for Ceramic Arts
19 Brick Hill Road
Newcastle, ME 04553
Phone: (207) 882-6075

Nevada

Tuscarora Pottery School
Box 7
Tuscarora, NV 89834
Phone: (702) 756-6598

New Jersey

Peters Valley Craft Center
19 Kuhn Road
Layton, NJ 07851
Phone: (201) 948-5200
Fax: (201) 948-0011

New York

Greenwich House Pottery
16 Jones Street
New York, NY 10014
Phone: (212) 242-4106

North Carolina

Penland School of Crafts
Penland Road
Penland, NC 28765
Phone: (704) 765-2359

Tennessee

Arrowmont School of Arts and Crafts
P.O. Box 567
Gatlinburg, TN 37738
Phone: (423) 436-5860
Fax: (423) 430-4101

Canada

Banff Centre for the Arts
Box 1020
Banff, Alberta T0L 0C0
Phone: (403) 762-6180

Metchosin International School of Art
RR #1
Pearson College
Victoria, British Columbia V9B 5T7
Phone: (250) 391-2420
Fax: (250) 391-2412

Artsperience
Canadore College
100 College Drive
North Bay, Ontario P1B 8K9
Phone: (705) 474-7600 ext. 5385
Fax: (705) 494-7462

Great Britain

Brunel University Arts Centre
Uxbridge, Middlesex UB8 3PH
Phone: (895) 273482
Fax: (895) 203250

Video

Jatun Molino: A Pottery Village in the Upper Amazon Basin is a video documentary that depicts the daily life and pottery techniques of the Quechua Indians who live in Jatun Molino. It is available from Joseph Molinaro, 319 Linden Walk, Lexington, Kentucky, 40508.

Directory of Artists

Ah-Leon
5F #11 Lang 219 Sec. 3
Kang-Ning Road 11422
Taipei, Taiwan

Jim Connell
355 E. Main Street
Rock Hill, South Carolina
29730

Stanley Mace Andersen
Route 3, Box 67
Bakersville, North Carolina
28705

Malcolm Davis
2322 Nineteenth Street, NW
Washington, D.C.
20009

Linda Arbuckle
Route 1, Box 206
Micanopy, Florida
32667

Eleanora Eden
Paradise Hill
Bellows Falls, Vermont
05101

Linda Christianson
35801 Vibo Trail
Lindstrom, Minnesota
55045

Frank Fabens
310 NW 40th, Suite D
Seattle, Washington
98107

Michelle Coakes
302 Patriot Court
Louisville, Kentucky
40214

Steven Hill
7212 Washington
Kansas City, Missouri
64114

Nick Joerling
Box 147
Penland, North Carolina
28765

Davie Reneau
2932 Woodscreek Road
Liberty, Kentucky
42539

Suze Lindsay
RR 1, Box 164A
Bakersville, North Carolina
28705

Michael Simon
Route 1, Box 35
Colbert, Georgia
30628

Joe Molinaro
319 Linden Walk
Lexington, Kentucky
40508

Chris Staley
120 W. Lytle
State College, Pennsylvania
16801

Peter Pinnell
2102 Lake Street
Lincoln, Nebraska
68502

Lana Wilson
465 Hidden Pines Lane
Del Mar, California
92014

Sally Porter
5668 Monckes Road
Colgate, Wisconsin
53017

Photo Credits

Page 8: *Tall Persian Jar with Fish Decoration,* by Michael Simon. Photo by Walker Montgomery.

Page 10: Photo of cupboard by Michelle Coakes.

Page 14: *Nesting Batter Bowls,* by Chris Staley. Photo by artist.

Stanley Mace Anderson
Tureen & Plate, Wall Platter, Vase
Photos by Tom Mills

Linda Arbuckle
Biscuit Jar with Lateral Leaves, Oval Footed Platter with Lateral Leaves, Spring in Mardi Gras Teapot, Footed Oval: Chartreuse, Shape of Spring Teapot, Gloriosa Teapot, Footed Boat: Wisteria, Biscuit Jar: Plenty
Photos by Linda Arbuckle

Linda Christianson
Five Square Plates, Oil Cans, Oval Baker, Teapot, Vase, Pitcher
Photos by Linda Christianson

Jim Connell
Copper Green Carved Lidded Jar, Copper Green Carved Pitcher, Copper Green Carved Vases
Photos by Paula Smith and Jim Connell

Malcolm Davis
Shino Tea Bowl, Faceted Jar, Teapot with Feet
Photos by Malcolm Davis

Eleanora Eden
Tripoidal Lidded Cauldron, Lidded Ewer
Photos by George Leisey

Frank Fabens
Tall B Vase, Teapot
Photos by Tom Holt

Steven Hill
Platter, Cypress Ewer, Melon Pitcher
Photos by Al Surratt

Jatun Molino
Chicha jar, Mucaua, Tinajas, Juri-Juri, Ecuadorian potter holds finished vase, Chicha fermenting jars
Photos by Joseph Molinaro

Nick Joerling
Teapots, Cream & Sugar & Tray
Photos by Tom Mills

Suze Lindsay
*Raised Square Platter, Margarita
Pitcher and Tumblers*
Photos by Tom Mills

Joseph Molinaro
Pitcher, Cup
Photos by Joseph Molinaro

Peter Pinnell
Teapot (pages 77 and 78)
Photos by Peter Pinnell

Sally Porter
*Oval Vase Form, Vase Form with Rope
Lip and Foot*
Photos by William Lemke

Davie Marie Reneau
Pitcher, Three Bottles
Photos by Davie Reneau

Michael Simon
*Persian Jar, Two Cups, Donut Bottle,
Pitcher with Pulled Lip, Tall Persian
Jar with Fish Decoration*
Photos by Walker Montgomery

Chris Staley
*Nesting Batter Bowls, Black Clay
Covered Jar, Four Cups* (page 34), *Four
Cups* (page 46), *Four Cups* (page 47),
Square Covered Jar
Photos by Chris Staley

Lana Wilson
*Ceremonial Teapot, Ritual Teapot, Altar
Teapot, Ceremonial Bowl*
Photos by John Dixon

Index

About the Author

Potter, teacher, and writer, Michelle Coakes directs the ceramics program at the University of Louisville. She has previously taught at Western Kentucky University, Florida Gulf Coast Art Center, Appalachian Center for Crafts, and Arrowmont School. Coakes has written about pottery for such publications as *Ceramics Monthly* and *NCECA Journal*. She also exhibits her own ceramic work.

∧ *Anagama Vase with Rings*

by MICHELLE COAKES
Stoneware
14" x 5" diameter (36 cm x 13 cm)

∧ *Stacked Vase*

by MICHELLE COAKES
Stoneware
12" x 5" diameter (30 cm x 13 cm)